101 MOCKTAILS RECIPE BOOK

Flavorful Non-Alcoholic Drinks for Any Occasion. Classic Favorites, Healthy Boosters, Exotic Creations, and Brunch Delights

Jeffrey C. Chapman

Designed by Mariska Kiesel

Table of Contents

Introduction

Dear fellow sippers and mixology enthusiasts!

Let's be honest—for a long time, "non-alcoholic drink" usually meant a sad glass of soda water or (gasp!) plain juice at a party. But not anymore. We're in the midst of a full-blown mocktail revolution, and I, for one, couldn't be more thrilled.

For me, it started with deciding to cut back on alcohol, which always made me feel lousy afterward. Whatever the reason, I dove headfirst into the world of flavor combinations, learned to muddle with the best of them, and realized that alcohol-free doesn't have to mean flavor-free. In fact, it often means the opposite!

So, whether you're "sober curious," a dedicated teetotaler, a party host extraordinaire, or just someone who wants to enjoy a tasty beverage without the next-day regret, this book is for you. Inside, you'll find a collection of drool-worthy mocktail recipes, tips to impress your friends, and everything you need to become your own master mixologist – no alcohol required.

Get ready to raise your glass (filled with something delicious, of course!). The zero-proof party is about to begin!

Raise Your Glass - The Allure of Going Alcohol-Free

Remember that time when ordering a "mocktail" meant getting a sugary concoction that tasted vaguely of childhood and disappointment? Yeah, me too. But thankfully, those days are long gone.

Today, opting for alcohol-free is cool, it's conscious, and it's downright delicious. We're witnessing a seismic shift in the way people drink, with a global movement embracing the sophisticated, flavorful world of non-alcoholic beverages.

The Mocktail Explosion: A Global Phenomenon

This isn't just a passing trend. The numbers speak for themselves:

- **Market Growth:** The global non-alcoholic beverage market is experiencing explosive growth.
- **Millennials Leading the Charge:** Okay, maybe this is partly about trends, but in the best way possible! Younger generations are driving the demand for healthier and more mindful drinking choices, and mocktails fit the bill perfectly.
- **Beyond the Bar:** It's not just happening in restaurants and bars. Supermarkets are dedicating more shelf space to alcohol-free options, and online retailers report booming sales of zero-proof spirits, mixers, and cocktail kits.

So, What's Fueling This Alcohol-Free Revolution?

The reasons are as diverse as the people raising their alcohol-free glasses:

- **Health & Wellness:** More and more people are paying attention to their well-being. Cutting back on alcohol is a simple way to reduce sugar intake, improve sleep, boost energy levels, and feel healthier overall.
- **Social Inclusion:** Mocktails level the playing field, offering an inclusive option for everyone at gatherings, whether they choose to drink alcohol or not.
- **Expanding Palates:** Let's face it, a well-crafted mocktail is a thing of beauty. Forget the boring beverages of the past—today's mocktails are all about exploring unique flavor combinations, experimenting with fresh ingredients, and delighting your taste buds in new and exciting ways.

The Bottom Line? This is just the beginning. The zero-proof movement is here to stay, offering a refreshing and flavorful alternative in a world often saturated with alcohol. So, whether you're a long-time teetotaler or just starting to explore the world of alcohol-free drinks, get ready to discover a world of delicious possibilities!

More Than Just a Fad: The Real Benefits of Choosing Zero-Proof

Sure, mocktails are having their moment in the spotlight—but look beyond the trend, and you'll find benefits that run deeper than a hashtag. Choosing to go alcohol-free, even occasionally, can have a seriously positive impact on your life:

Hello, Healthier You!

Let's be real, alcohol isn't exactly known for its health benefits. By swapping out those booze-filled drinks for refreshing mocktails, you're automatically making a healthier choice. This means:

- **Reduced Sugar Intake:** Say goodbye to those sugary mixers and syrups often found in alcoholic cocktails. Mocktails can be just as delicious with natural sweeteners like fruit, herbs, and spices.

- **Calorie Control:** Alcoholic drinks can be surprisingly high in calories. Mocktails offer a guilt-free way to enjoy a flavorful drink without derailing your healthy eating plans.
- **Better Sleep:** Alcohol might make you feel sleepy, but it actually disrupts the quality of your sleep. Mocktails, on the other hand, won't leave you feeling groggy or sleep-deprived.

Social Butterfly, Unleashed!

One of the best things about mocktails?
They're for everyone! This means:

- **Inclusivity:** Mocktails create a welcoming atmosphere for everyone at gatherings, regardless of whether they choose to drink alcohol or not. Pregnant women, designated drivers, those who abstain for personal or religious reasons—everyone can join in on the fun!
- **Clearer Connections:** Without alcohol clouding your judgment and lowering inhibitions, you're free to socialize with clarity and really connect with the people around you.

More Than Just a Drink:

Choosing mocktails can be a powerful act of self-care and mindful living:

- **Taking Control:** In a world where alcohol is often the default, opting for a mocktail is a way to challenge those norms and prioritize your well-being.
- **Newfound Freedom:** No more worrying about hangovers, making impulsive decisions, or feeling pressured to keep up with the crowd.

So, the next time you're out with friends, hosting a party, or just need a refreshing drink at home, remember: Choosing a mocktail isn't just trendy—it's a toast to a healthier, happier, and more mindful you.

Beyond Soda & Water: Where Mocktails Become an Art Form

Gone are the days when "alcohol-free" conjured images of boring beverages and Shirley Temples (although we did include a few classic drinks here as well). Get ready to be wowed, because modern mocktails are all about flavor, innovation, and pure drinking pleasure:

A Symphony of Flavors: The beauty of mocktails is that you're free to let your taste buds be your guide. Think:

Fresh, Seasonal Ingredients: Imagine muddled berries bursting with summer sunshine, crisp cucumber and mint awakened with a squeeze of lime, or warming spices that evoke cozy winter nights.

Exotic Inspirations: From tangy tamarind to floral hibiscus to smoky mezcal-inspired agave syrups, mocktails embrace global flavors for a taste bud adventure.

Unexpected Twists: Who says mocktails can't be sophisticated? We're talking infused waters with herbs and fruits, shrubs (drinking vinegars) that add a tangy punch, and homemade bitters that rival any craft cocktail bar creation.

Master Mixologist, At Your Service (It's You!):

Forget about complicated recipes with a million ingredients. Mocktails can be as simple or as elaborate as you like. You'll find options for every skill level, from quick and easy recipes to more adventurous creations that will unleash your inner mixologist.

The Art of Presentation: Let's be honest, half the fun of a great drink is how stunning it looks! Mocktails are all about:

Gorgeous Glassware: Don't underestimate the power of a beautiful coupe glass, vintage tumbler, or mason jar to elevate your drinking experience.

Garnishing with Flair: Fresh herbs, citrus twists, edible flowers, and even creatively carved fruits add visual appeal and aromatic delight.

Ready to Raise Your Glass? The world of mocktails is brimming with delicious possibilities. This book is your passport to exciting flavors, endless creativity, and a new appreciation for the art of crafting and savoring a truly exceptional drink—no alcohol required.

Your Home Mocktail Bar Tools & Techniques

Ready to transform your kitchen into a haven of zero-proof deliciousness? It's easier than you think! You don't need a fancy bar setup to craft incredible mocktails at home. With just a few key tools and a dash of enthusiasm, you'll be shaking and stirring like a pro in no time.

Essential Tools: Equipping Your Mocktail Arsenal

Cocktail Shaker: Your trusty sidekick for countless mocktail creations. A shaker is essential for chilling and combining ingredients, creating that perfectly integrated flavor you crave.

- *Types:* The classic Cobbler shaker (the one with the built-in strainer) is a great starter option. If you're serious about your mixology, consider adding a Boston shaker (two-piece shaker with a mixing glass and metal tin), which allows for greater control and faster chilling.

Jigger: Eyeballing measurements is so last year! A jigger ensures precision pouring, guaranteeing consistent results and preventing any accidental over-pouring (we've all been there!).

- Sizes: Look for a jigger with both a 1-ounce and 2-ounce side for maximum versatility.

Muddler: Release the flavors! A muddler is used to crush fruits, herbs, and spices, extracting their essence and adding a vibrant punch to your drinks.

- Material Matters: Opt for a muddler made of wood or stainless steel, as they're durable and won't impart any unwanted flavors.

Strainer: Say goodbye to unwanted bits and pieces in your drink. A strainer is crucial for creating smooth, refined cocktails.

- Must-Haves: A Hawthorne strainer (the one with the spring) is perfect for most shaking tasks, while a fine-mesh strainer will come in handy for double-straining those extra-smooth mocktails.

Bar Spoon: This isn't just any spoon – its long handle and special design are perfect for layering drinks and gently stirring delicate mixtures.

Citrus Juicer: Freshly squeezed citrus juice is non-negotiable for vibrant, flavorful mocktails. Invest in a good-quality citrus juicer (handheld or electric) and taste the difference.

Cutting Board and Knife: From slicing fruit garnishes to prepping herbs, a sharp knife and sturdy cutting board are your prep work heroes.

The Shake

Your go-to move for chilled, mixed-to-perfection mocktails. Here's the shake-down:

1. Fill It: Add all ingredients (except for sparkling beverages or garnishes) to your cocktail shaker. Don't forget the ice—it's crucial for proper chilling and dilution.

2. Seal It Tight: Secure the lid on your shaker, making sure it's nice and snug.

3. Shake It Like You Mean It: Hold the shaker with both hands and shake vigorously for 15-20 seconds, or until the outside of the shaker is frosty. (This is also a great stress reliever!)

4. Strain Like a Pro: Hold your Hawthorne strainer over a chilled glass and pour your perfectly mixed mocktail.

The Muddle

Time to release those fresh flavors! Muddling is all about gently crushing ingredients to extract their essence, not pulverizing them into oblivion. Here's how:

1. Prep Your Ingredients: Gently bruise ingredients like herbs or fruit slices with the back of a spoon to help release their flavors.

2. Muddle with Care: Place the prepped ingredients in the bottom of your shaker or mixing glass. Press down on them with your muddler and gently twist, repeating a few times. Remember, the goal is to extract flavor, not turn your ingredients to mush!

The Layer

For beautifully layered drinks that wow with their visual appeal, mastering the art of layering is key.

1. Density is Your Friend: Start with the densest ingredient (like syrups or purees) and work your way up to the least dense (like alcohol-free spirits or juices).

2. The Slow Pour: Use the back of a bar spoon to gently pour each layer over the previous one. Hold the spoon close to the surface of the drink to help prevent the layers from mixing.

3. Practice Makes Perfect: Layering takes a bit of practice, so don't be discouraged if your first few attempts aren't flawless.

4. Pro Tip: Have fun experimenting with different techniques and combinations! Mixology is all about creativity and discovering new flavors you love.

Pro Tips: Elevate Your Mocktail Game

Want to take your mocktails from good to "Wow, did you make this?!" Here are some tips and tricks to impress even the most discerning palate:

1. **Fresh is Best (Seriously):** Whenever possible, use fresh, high-quality ingredients. Freshly squeezed citrus juice, ripe fruits, and vibrant herbs will make a world of difference in the flavor of your mocktails.

2. **Ice Matters:** Don't underestimate the power of good ice! Use large ice cubes (or spheres) in your cocktails—they melt slower, preventing dilution and keeping your drinks colder for longer.

3. **Sweet Talk:** Balance is key in mixology. If a drink is too sweet, add a squeeze of citrus juice or a splash of unsweetened soda water. If it's too tart, add a touch of simple syrup or agave nectar.

4. **Taste as You Go:** Just like a chef tastes their food while cooking, a good mixologist tastes their creations as they go. This allows you to adjust flavors and ensure everything is perfectly balanced. (And who doesn't love a little taste test?)

5. **Chill Out:** A chilled glass makes all the difference. Before mixing your drink, pop your glasses in the freezer for a few minutes to achieve that frosty, inviting look.

6. **Garnish with Purpose:** Garnishes aren't just for show—they add an extra layer of flavor and aroma to your drinks. Choose garnishes that complement the flavors in your mocktail and add a pop of color or visual interest.

7. **Don't Be Afraid to Experiment:** The beauty of mocktails is that there are endless possibilities for flavor combinations! Get creative, experiment with different ingredients, and don't be afraid to step outside of your comfort zone. You might just invent your new signature drink!

8. **Have Fun!** Mixing mocktails should be enjoyable. Relax, put on some music, and let your creativity flow. The more fun you have, the more delicious your drinks will be.

Preparing Simple Syrup: The Sweet Foundation of Mocktails

As we delve deeper into the art of crafting delicious mocktails, it's important to highlight the foundational elements that make these beverages truly shine. One such element is the simple syrup, a versatile and essential ingredient that adds sweetness and balance to many of your favorite drinks. Understanding how to prepare and use simple syrup will elevate your mixology skills and ensure that every mocktail you create is perfectly balanced and irresistibly delicious.

Simple syrup is incredibly easy to make and can be customized with various flavors to complement the ingredients in your mocktails. Here's a basic recipe to get you started:

Basic Simple Syrup Recipe

Ingredients:

- 1 cup of granulated sugar
- 1 cup of water

Steps:

1. Combine the sugar and water in a saucepan.

2. Heat the mixture over medium heat, stirring constantly until the sugar is completely dissolved.

3. Once dissolved, remove the saucepan from the heat and let the syrup cool.

4. Transfer the cooled syrup to a clean glass jar or bottle and store it in the refrigerator. It will keep for about a month.

With your simple syrup ready, you're well on your way to crafting a variety of delightful and refreshing mocktails. Whether you're preparing a classic Virgin Mojito, a sophisticated Lavender Lemon Berry Cooler, or a fruity Tropical Sunrise Fizz, the addition of simple syrup will enhance the flavors and bring your drinks to the next level.

Variations:

Vanilla Simple Syrup: Add a vanilla bean split lengthwise or 1 teaspoon of vanilla extract to the basic recipe.

Herbal Simple Syrup: Add a handful of fresh herbs such as mint, basil, or rosemary during the heating process, then strain the syrup before storing.

Citrus Simple Syrup: Add the zest of a lemon, lime, or orange during the heating process, then strain the syrup before storing.

Confident Hosting: Throwing a Zero-Proof Party to Remember

Who says you need alcohol to get the party started? Hosting an alcohol-free event is a wonderful way to create a welcoming, inclusive atmosphere where everyone can let loose and enjoy themselves (without the hangover).

Here's how to plan a zero-proof bash that will have your guests saying, "Wait, there's no alcohol in these drinks?!" (in the best way possible, of course):

1. **Set the Tone (and Manage Expectations):**
   - Spread the Word (Subtly): Let guests know in advance that it's an alcohol-free affair. You can casually mention it in your invitations ("Join me for a fun and refreshing mocktail party!") or social media posts.
   - Focus on the Experience: Emphasize the other elements that will make your gathering amazing—delicious food, great music, fun activities, good company. It's about creating a vibe, not relying on booze.

2. Create a Mocktail Oasis:

- Variety is Key: Offer a selection of at least 3-4 different mocktail options to cater to different taste preferences. Consider having a mix of fruity, refreshing, and perhaps a slightly more "sophisticated" option (like a mocktail with herbal or spicy notes).
- DIY Delight: Set up a fun "make-your-own mocktail" station with various mixers, syrups, fresh herbs, and garnishes. Let your guests channel their inner mixologist!
- Presentation Matters: Just because it's alcohol-free doesn't mean it can't be fancy! Invest in some fun glassware, ice molds, and garnishes to elevate the visual appeal of your drinks.

3. Food, Glorious Food!

- Flavors to Impress: Serve food that complements your mocktail offerings. Think bright, fresh dishes, flavorful appetizers, and sweet treats.
- Timing is Everything: Ensure there are snacks available throughout the evening to keep those energy levels up (and avoid any potential "hanger" situations).

4. Entertainment Elevated:

- Beyond the Booze: Plan activities to keep the energy upbeat and the conversation flowing—think board games, card games, karaoke, a themed playlist, or even a DIY craft project.

5. Embrace the Early Finish:

- No Pressure, No Problem: Don't feel pressured to keep the party going until the wee hours of the morning. Without alcohol involved, people might be perfectly content to enjoy a delightful evening and head home at a reasonable hour (imagine that!).
- Most Importantly: Be yourself, be a gracious host, and have fun! When you approach your alcohol-free party with enthusiasm and creativity, your guests will feed off that energy and have a blast, regardless of what's in their glass.

Blackberry Basil Limeade

Fruity Mocktails

Watermelon Jalapeno Cooler

Tropical Sunrise Fiz

Description:

This vibrant mocktail combines the sweetness of mango with the tartness of passion fruit, balanced by coconut water and brightened with a splash of lime. The addition of sparkling water gives it a refreshing fizz.

Calories - 120

Ingredients:

- 2 oz mango puree
- 1 oz passion fruit juice
- 3 oz coconut water
- 1/2 oz lime juice
- 2 oz sparkling water
- Ice
- Mango slice and mint sprig for garnish

Low Calorie Alternative:

Use light coconut water and reduce mango puree to 1 oz.

Steps:

1. In a shaker, combine mango puree, passion fruit juice, coconut water, and lime juice with ice.

2. Shake vigorously for 10-15 seconds. Strain into a tall glass filled with ice.

3. Top with sparkling water and stir gently. Garnish with a mango slice and mint sprig.

Serving Suggestions:

Serve in a tall hurricane glass with a colorful paper straw.

Lavender Lemon Berry Cooler

Description:

This sophisticated mocktail combines the floral notes of lavender with the brightness of lemon and the sweetness of mixed berries. The honey adds depth, while the soda water provides a refreshing fizz.

Calories - 150

Ingredients:

- 1 oz lavender simple syrup
- 1 oz lemon juice
- 2 oz mixed berry puree (strawberries, raspberries, and blueberries)
- 1/2 oz honey
- 3 oz soda water
- Ice
- Fresh berries and lavender sprig for garnish

Steps:

1. In a shaker, combine lavender syrup, lemon juice, berry puree, and honey with ice.

2. Shake well for 10-15 seconds. Strain into a glass filled with ice.

3. Top with soda water and stir gently. Garnish with fresh berries and a lavender sprig.

Low Calorie Alternative:

Use a sugar-free lavender syrup and replace honey with a zero-calorie sweetener.

Serving Suggestions:

Serve in a wine glass or a stemless goblet.

Cucumber Mint Melon Refresher

Description:

This light and refreshing mocktail combines the crispness of cucumber with the sweetness of honeydew melon and the cooling effect of mint. A touch of elderflower cordial adds complexity.

Ingredients:

- 3 oz honeydew melon juice
- 1 oz cucumber juice
- 1/2 oz elderflower cordial
- 6-8 mint leaves
- 2 oz coconut water
- Ice
- Cucumber ribbon and mint sprig for garnish

Calories - 70

Low Calorie Alternative:

Use a sugar-free lavender syrup and replace honey with a zero-calorie sweetener.

Serving Suggestions:

Serve in a wine glass or a stemless goblet.

Steps:

1. In a mixing glass, muddle mint leaves gently.
2. Add honeydew juice, cucumber juice, elderflower cordial, and coconut water.
3. Fill with ice and stir well for 20-30 seconds.
4. Strain into a glass filled with fresh ice. Garnish with a cucumber ribbon and mint sprig.

Spiced Pineapple Ginger Zinger

Description:

This bold mocktail combines the tropical sweetness of pineapple with the warmth of ginger and a hint of cinnamon. A splash of lime adds brightness, while club soda gives it a lively fizz.

Ingredients:

- 3 oz pineapple juice
- 1 oz ginger syrup
- 1/4 tsp ground cinnamon
- 1/2 oz lime juice
- 2 oz club soda
- Ice
- Pineapple wedge and crystallized ginger for garnish

Calories - 130

Steps:

1. In a shaker, combine pineapple juice, ginger syrup, cinnamon, and lime juice with ice.

2. Shake vigorously for 10-15 seconds. Strain into a glass filled with ice.

3. Top with club soda and stir gently. Garnish with a pineapple wedge and a piece of crystallized ginger.

Low Calorie Alternative:

Use light pineapple juice and a sugar-free ginger syrup.

Serving Suggestions:

Serve in a tiki glass or a mason jar.

Rosemary Grapefruit Sparkler

Description:

This sophisticated mocktail balances the tartness of grapefruit with the herbal notes of rosemary. A touch of honey adds sweetness, while tonic water provides a pleasant bitterness and effervescence.

Calories - 140

Ingredients:

- 3 oz fresh grapefruit juice
- 1 oz rosemary simple syrup
- 1/2 oz honey
- 2 oz tonic water
- Ice
- Grapefruit slice and rosemary sprig for garnish

Low Calorie Alternative:

Use a sugar-free rosemary syrup and replace honey with a zero-calorie sweetener.

Steps:

1. In a shaker, combine grapefruit juice, rosemary syrup, and honey with ice.

2. Shake well for 10-15 seconds. Strain into a glass filled with ice.

3. Top with tonic water and stir gently. Garnish with a grapefruit slice and a rosemary sprig.

Serving Suggestions:

Serve in a rocks glass or a coupe glass.

Blackberry Basil Limeade

Description:

This refreshing mocktail combines the tartness of lime with the sweetness of blackberries and the aromatic touch of basil. The result is a perfectly balanced, visually striking drink.

Calories - 100

Ingredients:

- 8-10 fresh blackberries
- 5-6 basil leaves
- 2 oz lime juice
- 1 oz simple syrup
- 3 oz sparkling water
- Ice
- Blackberry and basil leaf for garnish

Low Calorie Alternative:

Use a zero-calorie sweetener instead of simple syrup.

Steps:

1. In a shaker, muddle blackberries and basil leaves. Add lime juice, simple syrup, and ice.

2. Shake vigorously for 15 seconds. Double strain into a glass filled with ice.

3. Top with sparkling water and stir gently. Garnish with a blackberry and basil leaf.

Serving Suggestions:

Serve in a rocks glass with a metal straw.

Peach Vanilla Cream Soda

Description:

This creamy mocktail combines the sweetness of peaches with the warmth of vanilla. The addition of cream soda gives it a nostalgic touch and a smooth, velvety texture.

Ingredients:

- 3 oz peach puree
- 1/2 tsp vanilla extract
- 1 oz half-and-half
- 3 oz cream soda
- Ice
- Peach slice for garnish

Calories - 180

Steps:

1. In a shaker, combine peach puree, vanilla extract, and half-and-half with ice.

2. Shake well for 10-15 seconds. Strain into a glass filled with ice.

3. Top with cream soda and stir gently. Garnish with a peach slice.

Low Calorie Alternative:

Use sugar-free cream soda and replace half-and-half with almond milk.

Serving Suggestions:

Serve in a tall glass with a wide straw.

Matcha Kiwi Cooler

Description:

This unique mocktail combines the earthy flavor of matcha with the tangy sweetness of kiwi. A splash of coconut water adds tropical notes, while mint provides a refreshing finish.

Calories - 130

Ingredients:

- 1 tsp matcha powder
- 1 oz hot water
- 2 kiwis, peeled and chopped
- 1 oz simple syrup
- 2 oz coconut water
- 5-6 mint leaves
- Ice
- Kiwi slice and mint sprig for garnish

Steps:

1. Dissolve matcha powder in hot water, then let it cool.
2. In a shaker, muddle kiwi and mint leaves.
3. Add cooled matcha, simple syrup, coconut water, and ice.
4. Shake vigorously for 15 seconds.
5. Double strain into a glass filled with ice. Garnish with a kiwi slice and mint sprig.

Low Calorie Alternative:

Use a zero-calorie sweetener instead of simple syrup.

Serving Suggestions:

Serve in a double old-fashioned glass.

Blood Orange Cardamom Fizz

Description:

This sophisticated mocktail combines the unique flavor of blood oranges with the warm, spicy notes of cardamom. A splash of tonic water adds bitterness and effervescence.

Calories - 120

Ingredients:

- 3 oz blood orange juice
- 1 oz cardamom simple syrup
- 1/2 oz lemon juice
- 2 oz tonic water
- Ice
- Blood orange wheel and star anise for garnish

Low Calorie Alternative:

Use a sugar-free cardamom syrup and diet tonic water.

Steps:

1. In a shaker, combine blood orange juice, cardamom syrup, and lemon juice with ice.

2. Shake well for 10-15 seconds. Strain into a glass filled with ice.

3. Top with tonic water and stir gently. Garnish with a blood orange wheel and star anise.

Serving Suggestions:

Serve in a collins glass with a paper straw.

Lychee Rose Sparkler

Description:

This elegant mocktail combines the delicate sweetness of lychee with the floral notes of rose water. Sparkling water adds a refreshing fizz, while a hint of lime balances the flavors.

Calories - 110

Ingredients:

- 3 oz lychee juice
- 1/4 tsp rose water
- 1/2 oz lime juice
- 1 oz simple syrup
- 2 oz sparkling water
- Ice
- Lychee fruit and rose petal for garnish

Steps:

1. In a shaker, combine lychee juice, rose water, lime juice, and simple syrup with ice.

2. Shake gently for 10 seconds. Strain into a glass filled with ice.

3. Top with sparkling water and stir gently. Garnish with a lychee fruit and rose petal.

Low Calorie Alternative:

Use a zero-calorie sweetener instead of simple syrup.

Serving Suggestions:

Serve in a champagne flute or coupe glass.

Watermelon Jalapeno Cooler

Description:

This spicy-sweet mocktail combines the refreshing taste of watermelon with the kick of jalapeño. Lime adds brightness, while mint provides a cooling counterpoint to the heat.

Calories - 130

Ingredients:

- 3 oz fresh watermelon juice
- 1/4 jalapeño, seeds removed and sliced
- 1 oz lime juice
- 1 oz agave nectar
- 5-6 mint leaves
- 2 oz club soda
- Ice
- Watermelon wedge and jalapeño slice for garnish

Steps:

1. In a shaker, muddle jalapeño slices and mint leaves.
2. Add watermelon juice, lime juice, and agave nectar with ice.
3. Shake vigorously for 15 seconds. Double strain into a glass filled with ice.
4. Top with club soda and stir gently. Garnish with a watermelon wedge and jalapeño slice.

Low Calorie Alternative:

Use a zero-calorie sweetener instead of agave nectar.

Serving Suggestions:

Serve in a mason jar with a metal straw.

Fig & Thyme Sparkler

Description:

This sophisticated mocktail combines the subtle sweetness of figs with the earthy notes of thyme. A splash of balsamic vinegar adds depth, while prosecco-style sparkling grape juice provides elegance and effervescence.

Calories - 150

Ingredients:

- 2 fresh figs, quartered
- 2-3 thyme sprigs
- 1 oz simple syrup
- 1/2 oz lemon juice
- 1/4 tsp balsamic vinegar
- 3 oz alcohol-free prosecco or sparkling white grape juice
- Ice
- Fig slice and thyme sprig for garnish

Steps:

1. In a shaker, muddle figs, thyme leaves (from 1-2 sprigs), and simple syrup.
2. Add lemon juice, balsamic vinegar, and ice.
3. Shake well for 15 seconds. Double strain into a glass filled with ice.
4. Top with alcohol-free prosecco or sparkling grape juice. Garnish with a fig slice and thyme sprig.

Low Calorie Alternative:

Use a zero-calorie sweetener instead of simple syrup and choose a low-calorie sparkling grape juice.

Serving Suggestions:

Serve in a wine glass or champagne flute.

Pomegranate Chai Cider

Description:

This warming mocktail combines the tangy sweetness of pomegranate with the spicy notes of chai tea. Apple cider adds depth, while a cinnamon stick garnish enhances the aromatic experience.

Calories - 140

Ingredients:

- 2 oz pomegranate juice
- 2 oz strong-brewed chai tea, cooled
- 2 oz apple cider
- 1/2 oz honey
- 1/4 tsp lemon juice
- Ice
- Pomegranate seeds and cinnamon stick for garnish

Steps:

1. In a shaker, combine pomegranate juice, chai tea, apple cider, honey, and lemon juice with ice.
2. Shake well for 15 seconds. Strain into a glass filled with ice.
3. Garnish with pomegranate seeds and a cinnamon stick.

Low Calorie Alternative:

Use sugar-free apple cider and replace honey with a zero-calorie sweetener.

Serving Suggestions:

Serve in a mug or an irish coffee glass.

Dragon Fruit Mojito Mocktail

Description:

This visually stunning mocktail combines the subtle sweetness of dragon fruit with the classic mojito flavors of lime and mint. Coconut water adds tropical notes, while soda water provides a refreshing fizz.

Calories - 120

Ingredients:

- 1/2 dragon fruit, peeled and cubed
- 8-10 mint leaves
- 1 oz lime juice
- 1 oz simple syrup
- 2 oz coconut water
- 2 oz soda water
- Ice
- Dragon fruit slice and mint sprig for garnish

Low Calorie Alternative:

Use a zero-calorie sweetener instead of simple syrup.

Steps:

1. In a shaker, muddle dragon fruit cubes and mint leaves.
2. Add lime juice, simple syrup, and coconut water with ice.
3. Shake vigorously for 15 seconds. Strain into a glass filled with ice.
4. Top with soda water and stir gently. Garnish with a dragon fruit slice and mint sprig.

Serving Suggestions:

Serve in a highball glass with a bamboo straw.

Apricot Rosemary Honey Spritzer

Description:

This sophisticated mocktail combines the sweetness of apricots with the herbal notes of rosemary and the floral sweetness of honey. Sparkling water adds a refreshing fizz to balance the flavors.

Calories - 130

Ingredients:

- 2 oz apricot nectar
- 1 oz honey syrup (equal parts honey and hot water, cooled)
- 1/2 oz lemon juice
- 1 rosemary sprig
- 3 oz sparkling water
- Ice
- Apricot slice and rosemary sprig for garnish

Steps:

1. In a shaker, muddle the leaves from half the rosemary sprig.
2. Add apricot nectar, honey syrup, and lemon juice with ice.
3. Shake well for 15 seconds. Double strain into a glass filled with ice.
3. Top with sparkling water and stir gently. Garnish with an apricot slice and rosemary sprig.

Low Calorie Alternative:

Use sugar-free apricot nectar and replace honey syrup with a zero-calorie sweetener.

Serving Suggestions:

Serve in a white wine glass or a goblet.

Smoky Cactus Cooler

Description:

This unique mocktail combines the subtle flavor of prickly pear cactus with smoky lapsang souchong tea and a hint of lime. Agave nectar adds sweetness, while chili salt rim provides a spicy contrast.

Ingredients:

Calories - 100

- 2 oz prickly pear juice
- 1 oz cold-brewed lapsang souchong tea
- 1/2 oz lime juice
- 1/2 oz agave nectar
- 2 oz sparkling water
- Ice
- Chili salt for rim
- Prickly pear slice for garnish

Steps:

1. Rim glass with chili salt.

2. In a shaker, combine prickly pear juice, tea, lime juice, and agave nectar with ice.

3. Shake well and strain into the prepared glass over fresh ice.

4. Top with sparkling water and garnish with a prickly pear slice.

Low Calorie Alternative:

Use a zero-calorie sweetener instead of agave nectar.

Serving Suggestions:

Serve in a rocks glass with a chili-salt rim and a prickly pear slice for garnish.

Butterfly Pea Flower & Yuzu Fizz

Description:

This color-changing mocktail uses butterfly pea flower tea, which turns from blue to purple when mixed with citrus. Yuzu juice adds a unique citrus flavor, while egg white foam creates a luxurious texture.

Calories - 90

Ingredients:

- 2 oz butterfly pea flower tea
- 1 oz yuzu juice
- 1/2 oz simple syrup
- 1 egg white (or 1 oz aquafaba for vegan option)
- 2 oz tonic water
- Ice
- Edible flower for garnish

Low Calorie Alternative:

Use a zero-calorie sweetener instead of agave nectar.

Steps:

1. Dry shake egg white in a shaker without ice.

2. Add butterfly pea flower tea, yuzu juice, simple syrup, and ice. Shake vigorously. train into a glass without ice.

3. Slowly pour tonic water over a spoon to create a layered effect. Garnish with an edible flower.

Serving Suggestions:

Serve in a mug or an irish coffee glass.

Fermented Honey & Black Garlic Elixir

Description:

This savory-sweet mocktail combines the complex flavors of fermented honey and black garlic with the earthiness of beet juice. Apple cider vinegar adds tanginess, while rosemary provides an aromatic finish.

Calories - 90

Ingredients:

- 1 oz fermented honey
- 2 cloves black garlic, mashed
- 1 oz beet juice
- 1/2 oz apple cider vinegar
- 2 oz sparkling water
- Ice
- Rosemary sprig for garnish

Low Calorie Alternative:

Use a zero-calorie sweetener instead of fermented honey.

Steps:

1. In a shaker, muddle black garlic with fermented honey.

2. Add beet juice, apple cider vinegar, and ice. Shake well. Double strain into a glass filled with ice.

3. Top with sparkling water and stir gently. Garnish with a rosemary sprig.

Serving Suggestions:

Serve in a rocks glass with a rosemary sprig for garnish.

Durian & Jackfruit Tropical Splash

Description:

This bold mocktail combines the controversial durian fruit with the sweet jackfruit, balanced by coconut water and a touch of lime. Lemongrass adds a fresh, citrusy note.

Calories - 120

Ingredients:

- 1 oz durian puree
- 2 oz jackfruit juice
- 2 oz coconut water
- 1/2 oz lime juice
- 1 lemongrass stalk, bruised
- Ice
- Jackfruit slice for garnish

Steps:

1. In a shaker, combine durian puree, jackfruit juice, coconut water, and lime juice with ice.

2. Shake vigorously for 15 seconds. Strain into a glass filled with ice.

3. Garnish with a bruised lemongrass stalk and jackfruit slice.

Low Calorie Alternative:

Use a zero-calorie sweetener instead of agave nectar.

Serving Suggestions:

Serve in a highball glass with a lemongrass stalk and jackfruit slice for garnish.

Smoked Seaweed & Plum Wine Spritzer

Description:

This umami-rich mocktail combines the briny flavor of smoked seaweed with the sweetness of non-alcoholic plum wine. Yuzu bitters add complexity, while soda water provides effervescence.

Ingredients:

- 2 oz non-alcoholic plum wine
- 1/2 oz smoked seaweed syrup (seaweed-infused simple syrup)
- 3 dashes yuzu bitters
- 2 oz soda water
- Ice
- Nori strip for garnish

Calories - 70

Steps:

1. In a mixing glass, combine plum wine, seaweed syrup, and yuzu bitters with ice.

2. Stir well for 20 seconds. Strain into a glass filled with ice.

3. Top with soda water and stir gently. Garnish with a nori strip.

Low Calorie Alternative:
Use diet soda water.

Serving Suggestions:

Serve in a rocks glass with a nori strip for garnish.

Blue Algae Lemonade

Description:

This vibrant blue drink combines the earthy flavor of spirulina with tart lemonade and a hint of vanilla.

Calories - 100

Ingredients:

- 1 tsp blue spirulina powder
- 2 oz fresh lemon juice
- 1 oz vanilla syrup
- 3 oz coconut water
- Ice
- Lemon wheel and edible silver leaf for garnish

Steps:

1. In a shaker, combine spirulina, lemon juice, vanilla syrup, and coconut water.

2. Shake vigorously until spirulina is fully dissolved. Strain into a glass filled with ice.

3. Garnish with a lemon wheel and edible silver leaf.

Low Calorie Alternative:

Use a zero-calorie sweetener instead of vanilla syrup.

Serving Suggestions:

Serve in a tall glass with a lemon wheel and edible silver leaf for garnish.

Mushroom Chai Elixir

Description:

A savory-sweet mocktail that combines the earthiness of reishi mushroom with the warm spices of chai.

Calories - 70

Ingredients:

- 1 oz reishi mushroom tea concentrate
- 2 oz strong-brewed chai tea
- 1 oz oat milk
- 1/2 oz maple syrup
- Pinch of sea salt
- Ice
- Star anise for garnish

Low Calorie Alternative:

Use a zero-calorie sweetener instead of maple syrup.

Steps:

1. Combine all ingredients except garnish in a shaker with ice.

2. Shake well and strain into a glass filled with ice.

3. Garnish with star anise.

Serving Suggestions:

Serve in a mug with a star anise for garnish.

Avocado Matcha Frappe

Description:

A creamy, green drink that combines the richness of avocado with the earthy flavor of matcha.

Ingredients:

- 1/2 ripe avocado
- 1 tsp matcha powder
- 1 oz lime juice
- 1 oz agave nectar
- 4 oz coconut water
- Ice
- Matcha powder for dusting

Calories - 200

Steps:

1. Blend all ingredients until smooth.
2. Pour into a glass and dust with matcha powder.

Low Calorie Alternative:

Use a zero-calorie sweetener instead of agave nectar.

Serving Suggestions:

Serve in a smoothie glass with a matcha powder dusting for garnish.

Pickled Grape & Tarragon Fizz

Description:

A unique combination of pickled grapes and aromatic tarragon creates an intriguing flavor profile.

Ingredients:

- 3-4 pickled grapes, muddled
- 2-3 tarragon sprigs
- 1 oz white grape juice
- 1/2 oz pickle brine
- 3 oz tonic water
- Ice
- Pickled grape and tarragon sprig for garnish

Calories - 80

Steps:

1. Muddle pickled grapes and tarragon in a shaker.

2. Add grape juice, pickle brine, and ice. Shake well.

3. Double strain into a glass filled with ice. Top with tonic water and stir gently.

4. Garnish with a pickled grape and tarragon sprig.

Low Calorie Alternative:

Use a zero-calorie sweetener instead of pickle brine.

Serving Suggestions:

Serve in a highball glass with a pickled grape and tarragon sprig for garnish.

Smoked Tea & Pear Elixir

Description:

This sophisticated mocktail combines the smoky flavor of lapsang souchong tea with the sweetness of pear and a hint of rosemary.

Calories - 90

Ingredients:

- 2 oz cold-brewed lapsang souchong tea
- 1 oz pear nectar
- 1/2 oz rosemary syrup
- 1/4 oz lemon juice
- 2 oz sparkling water
- Ice
- Pear slice and rosemary sprig for garnish

Steps:

1. Combine tea, pear nectar, rosemary syrup, and lemon juice in a shaker with ice.
2. Shake well and strain into a glass filled with ice. Top with sparkling water and stir gently.
3. Garnish with a pear slice and rosemary sprig.

Low Calorie Alternative:

Use a zero-calorie sweetener instead of rosemary syrup.

Serving Suggestions:

Serve in a wine glass with a pear slice and rosemary sprig for garnish.

Beet & Black Garlic Tonic

Description:

A savory, earthy mocktail that combines the sweetness of beets with the complex flavor of black garlic.

Calories - 70

Ingredients:

- 2 oz beet juice
- 1/2 oz black garlic syrup (made by blending black garlic with simple syrup)
- 1/4 oz apple cider vinegar
- 3 oz tonic water
- Ice
- Beet chip and thyme sprig for garnish

Low Calorie Alternative:

Use a zero-calorie sweetener instead of black garlic syrup.

Steps:

1. Combine beet juice, black garlic syrup, and apple cider vinegar in a shaker with ice.

2. Shake well and strain into a glass filled with ice. Top with tonic water and stir gently.

3. Garnish with a beet chip and thyme sprig.

Serving Suggestions:

Serve in a rocks glass with a beet chip and thyme sprig for garnish.

Saffron & Cardamom Lassi

Description:

A luxurious, spiced mocktail inspired by the traditional Indian yogurt drink.

Ingredients:

- 3 oz plain yogurt
- 1 oz mango puree
- 1/4 tsp saffron threads, soaked in 1 tbsp warm water
- 1/4 tsp ground cardamom
- 1 oz honey
- 2 oz sparkling water
- Ice
- Pistachio slivers and edible gold leaf for garnish

Calories - 150

Steps:

1. Blend yogurt, mango puree, saffron with its soaking water, cardamom, and honey until smooth.

2. Pour over ice in a glass. Top with sparkling water and stir gently.

3. Garnish with pistachio slivers and edible gold leaf.

Low Calorie Alternative:

Use fat-free yogurt and a zero-calorie sweetener instead of honey.

Serving Suggestions:

Serve in a goblet with pistachio slivers and edible gold leaf for garnish.

Truffle & Porcini Martini

Description:

A savory, umami-rich mocktail that mimics the complexity of a dirty martini.

Ingredients:

- 2 oz porcini mushroom stock
- 1 oz olive brine
- 1/4 tsp truffle oil
- 2 dashes non-alcoholic bitters
- Ice
- Blue cheese-stuffed olive for garnish

Calories - 50

Steps:

1. Combine all ingredients except garnish in a mixing glass with ice.

2. Stir well for about 30 seconds. Strain into a chilled martini glass.

3. Garnish with a blue cheese-stuffed olive.

Low Calorie Alternative:

Use a zero-calorie sweetener instead of olive brine.

Serving Suggestions:

Serve in a martini glass with a blue cheese-stuffed olive for garnish.

Squid Ink & Yuzu Spritz

Description:

A dramatic black mocktail with a bright citrus flavor.

Calories - 60

Ingredients:

- 1/4 tsp food-grade squid ink
- 1 oz yuzu juice
- 1/2 oz simple syrup
- 3 oz sparkling water
- Ice
- Lemon twist for garnish

Low Calorie Alternative:

Use a zero-calorie sweetener instead of black garlic syrup.

Steps:

1. In a shaker, combine squid ink, yuzu juice, and simple syrup with ice.

2. Shake vigorously until well combined. Strain into a glass filled with ice.

3. Top with sparkling water and stir gently. Garnish with a lemon twist.

Serving Suggestions:

Serve in a rocks glass with a beet chip and thyme sprig for garnish.

Szechuan Button Buzz

Description:
This unique mocktail features the Szechuan button, a flower bud that creates a tingling sensation in the mouth.

Calories - 100

Ingredients:
- 2 oz lychee juice
- 1 oz lime juice
- 1/2 oz honey syrup
- 2 oz tonic water
- Ice
- 1 Szechuan button flower
- Lime wheel for garnish

Low Calorie Alternative:
Use a zero-calorie sweetener instead of honey syrup.

Serving Suggestions:
Serve in a rocks glass with a lime wheel and a Szechuan button flower for garnish.

Steps:

1. Combine lychee juice, lime juice, and honey syrup in a shaker with ice.

2. Shake well and strain into a glass filled with ice. Top with tonic water and stir gently.

3. Garnish with a lime wheel and place the Szechuan button flower on top.

4. Garnish with a lime wheel and place the Szechuan button flower on top.

Peach & Ginger Fizz

Low-Calorie Mocktails

Hibiscus Rose Cooler

Cucumber Mint Sparkler

Description:

A refreshing, light drink that combines the crispness of cucumber with the coolness of mint.

Calories - 20

Ingredients:

- 1/2 cucumber, sliced
- 5-6 mint leaves
- 1 oz lime juice
- 4 oz sparkling water
- Ice
- Cucumber slice and mint sprig for garnish

Serving Suggestions:

Serve in a highball glass with a cucumber slice and mint sprig for garnish.

Steps:

1. Muddle cucumber and mint leaves in a shaker.

2. Add lime juice and ice, shake well. Strain into a glass filled with ice.

3. Top with sparkling water and stir gently. Garnish with a cucumber slice and mint sprig.

Berry Basil Fizz

Description:

A fruity, herbaceous drink that's low in calories but high in flavor.

Calories - 25

Ingredients:

- 1/4 cup mixed berries (strawberries, raspberries, blueberries)
- 3-4 basil leaves
- 1/2 oz lemon juice
- 4 oz diet lemon-lime soda
- Ice
- Berry and basil leaf for garnish

Steps:

1. Muddle berries and basil in a shaker. Add lemon juice and ice, shake vigorously.
2. Double strain into a glass filled with ice. Top with diet lemon-lime soda.
3. Garnish with a berry and basil leaf.

Serving Suggestions:

Serve in a highball glass with a cucumber slice and mint sprig for garnish.

Ginger Lemon Zinger

Description:

A spicy, tangy drink that aids digestion and provides a refreshing kick.

Ingredients:

- 1 oz fresh ginger juice
- 1 oz lemon juice
- 1/2 tsp zero-calorie sweetener
- 4 oz sparkling water
- Ice
- Lemon wheel and ginger slice for garnish

Calories - 15

Steps:

1. In a shaker, combine ginger juice, lemon juice, and sweetener with ice.

2. Shake well for 10-15 seconds. Strain into a glass filled with ice.

3. Top with sparkling water and stir gently. Garnish with a lemon wheel and ginger slice.

Serving Suggestions:

Serve in a highball glass with a lemon wheel and ginger slice for garnish.

Watermelon Rosemary Cooler

Description:

A unique combination of sweet watermelon and aromatic rosemary creates a sophisticated low-calorie drink.

Ingredients:

- 3 oz fresh watermelon juice
- 1 sprig rosemary
- 1/2 oz lime juice
- 3 oz sparkling water
- Ice
- Watermelon triangle and rosemary sprig for garnish

Calories - 30

Steps:

1. Muddle rosemary in a shaker.

2. Add watermelon juice, lime juice, and ice. Shake well.

3. Double strain into a glass filled with ice. Top with sparkling water and stir gently.

4. Garnish with a watermelon triangle and rosemary sprig.

Serving Suggestions:

Serve in a highball glass with a watermelon triangle and rosemary sprig for garnish.

Green Tea Citrus Cooler

Description:

A refreshing, antioxidant-rich drink that combines the benefits of green tea with zesty citrus flavors.

Calories - 10

Ingredients:

- 3 oz cold green tea (unsweetened)
- 1/2 oz lemon juice
- 1/2 oz lime juice
- 1/4 tsp zero-calorie sweetener
- 2 oz sparkling water
- Ice
- Lemon and lime wheels for garnish

Steps:

1. In a shaker, combine green tea, lemon juice, lime juice, and sweetener with ice.

2. Shake well for 10-15 seconds. Strain into a glass filled with ice.

3. Top with sparkling water and stir gently. Garnish with lemon and lime wheels.

Serving Suggestions:

Serve in a highball glass with lemon and lime wheels for garnish.

Lavender Lemonade Spritzer

Description:

A floral and citrusy drink that's both refreshing and calming.

Calories - 5

Ingredients:

- 2 oz sugar-free lavender syrup
- 1 oz lemon juice
- 4 oz sparkling water
- Ice
- Lemon wheel and lavender sprig for garnish

Steps:

1. Combine lavender syrup and lemon juice in a glass filled with ice.
2. Top with sparkling water and stir gently.
3. Garnish with a lemon wheel and lavender sprig.

Serving Suggestions:

Serve in a tall glass with a lemon wheel and lavender sprig for garnish.

Spiced Tomato Refresher

Description:

A savory, low-calorie alternative to a Bloody Mary.

Ingredients:

- 4 oz low-sodium tomato juice
- 1/4 tsp Worcestershire sauce
- Dash of hot sauce
- 1/4 tsp horseradish
- Pinch of celery salt
- Pinch of black pepper
- Ice
- Celery stick and cherry tomato for garnish

Calories - 30

Steps:

1. Combine all ingredients except garnishes in a shaker with ice.

2. Shake well and strain into a glass filled with ice.

3. Garnish with a celery stick and cherry tomato.

Serving Suggestions:

Serve in a highball glass with a celery stick and cherry tomato for garnish.

Kiwi Basil Smash

Description:

A tart and herbaceous drink that's packed with vitamin C.

Ingredients:

- 1 kiwi, peeled and chopped
- 5-6 basil leaves
- 1/2 oz lime juice
- 4 oz sparkling water
- Ice
- Kiwi slice and basil leaf for garnish

Calories - 40

Steps:

1. Muddle kiwi and basil in a shaker. Add lime juice and ice, shake vigorously.

2. Double strain into a glass filled with ice. Top with sparkling water and stir gently.

3. Garnish with a kiwi slice and basil leaf.

Serving Suggestions:

Serve in a rocks glass with a kiwi slice and basil leaf for garnish.

Peach & Ginger Fizz

Description:

A fruity and spicy combination that's perfect for summer.

Calories - 15

Ingredients:

- 2 oz sugar-free peach syrup
- 1/2 oz fresh ginger juice
- 1/2 oz lemon juice
- 3 oz diet ginger ale
- Ice
- Peach slice and crystallized ginger for garnish

Serving Suggestions:

Serve in a highball glass with a peach slice and crystallized ginger for garnish.

Steps:

1. Combine peach syrup, ginger juice, and lemon juice in a shaker with ice.

2. Shake well and strain into a glass filled with ice.

3. Top with diet ginger ale and stir gently.

3. Garnish with a peach slice and piece of crystallized ginger.

Hibiscus Lime Cooler

Description:

A tangy, vibrant drink with a beautiful deep red color.

Calories - 10

Ingredients:

- 3 oz hibiscus tea (unsweetened)
- 1 oz lime juice
- 1/4 tsp zero-calorie sweetener
- 2 oz sparkling water
- Ice
- Lime wheel and hibiscus flower for garnish

Serving Suggestions:

Serve in a highball glass with a lime wheel and hibiscus flower for garnish.

Steps:

1. Combine hibiscus tea, lime juice, and sweetener in a shaker with ice.

2. Shake well and strain into a glass filled with ice.

3. Top with sparkling water and stir gently.

3. Garnish with a lime wheel and hibiscus flower.

Cucumber Aloe Vera Refresher

Description:

A hydrating and soothing drink that's perfect for hot days.

Ingredients:

- 2 oz cucumber juice
- 1 oz aloe vera juice
- 1/2 oz lime juice
- 3 oz sparkling water
- Ice
- Cucumber ribbon for garnish

Calories - 20

Steps:

1. Combine cucumber juice, aloe vera juice, and lime juice in a shaker with ice.

2. Shake well and strain into a glass filled with ice. Top with sparkling water and stir gently.

3. Garnish with a cucumber ribbon.

Serving Suggestions:

Serve in a tall glass with a cucumber ribbon for garnish.

Matcha Mint Iced Tea

Description:

A refreshing, antioxidant-rich drink with a caffeine boost.

Ingredients:

- 1 tsp matcha powder
- 4 oz cold water
- 5-6 mint leaves
- 1/4 tsp zero-calorie sweetener
- Ice
- Mint sprig for garnish

Calories - 5

Steps:

1. Whisk matcha powder with 1 oz hot water until smooth. In a shaker, muddle mint leaves with sweetener.

2. Add matcha mixture and remaining cold water with ice. Shake well.

3. Strain into a glass filled with ice. Garnish with a mint sprig.

Serving Suggestions:

Serve in a tall glass with a mint sprig for garnish.

Strawberry Rhubarb Spritzer

Description:

A tart and sweet combination that's low in calories but high in flavor.

Calories - 25

Ingredients:

- 2 oz sugar-free strawberry syrup
- 1 oz rhubarb puree
- 1/2 oz lemon juice
- 3 oz sparkling water
- Ice
- Strawberry slice and rhubarb ribbon for garnish

Serving Suggestions:

Serve in a highball glass with a strawberry slice and rhubarb ribbon for garnish.

Steps:

1. Combine strawberry syrup, rhubarb puree, and lemon juice in a shaker with ice.

2. Shake well and strain into a glass filled with ice.

3. Top with sparkling water and stir gently.

3. Garnish with a strawberry slice and rhubarb ribbon.

Pineapple Cilantro Cooler

Description:

A tropical drink with a herbal twist.

Calories - 50

Ingredients:

- 3 oz pineapple juice (unsweetened)
- 5-6 cilantro sprigs
- 1/2 oz lime juice
- 2 oz coconut water
- Ice
- Pineapple wedge and cilantro sprig for garnish

Serving Suggestions:

Serve in a highball glass with a pineapple wedge and cilantro sprig for garnish.

Steps:

1. Muddle cilantro in a shaker.
2. Add pineapple juice, lime juice, and ice. Shake well. Double strain into a glass filled with ice.
3. Top with coconut water and stir gently.
3. Garnish with a pineapple wedge and cilantro sprig.

Blackberry Sage Spritzer

Description:

A sophisticated, low-calorie drink with complex flavors.

Ingredients:

- 5-6 blackberries
- 2-3 sage leaves
- 1/2 oz lemon juice
- 1/4 tsp zero-calorie sweetener
- 4 oz sparkling water
- Ice
- Blackberry and sage leaf for garnish

Calories - 15

Steps:

1. Muddle blackberries and sage leaves in a shaker.
2. Add lemon juice, sweetener, and ice. Shake vigorously.
3. Double strain into a glass filled with ice. Top with sparkling water and stir gently.
4. Garnish with a blackberry and sage leaf.

Serving Suggestions:

Serve in a highball glass with a blackberry and sage leaf for garnish.

Blue Algae Lemonade

Rosemary & Olive Brine Sparkler

Savory
Mocktails

Tomato Basil Refresher

Tomato Basil Refresher

Description:

A light, garden-fresh take on a Bloody Mary.

Calories - 70

Ingredients:

- 3 oz fresh tomato juice
- 1 oz basil simple syrup
- 1/2 oz lemon juice
- 2 dashes Worcestershire sauce
- Pinch of salt and black pepper
- 2 oz soda water
- Ice
- Cherry tomato and basil leaf for garnish

Steps:

1. Combine all ingredients except soda water in a shaker with ice.

2. Shake well and strain into a glass filled with ice. Top with soda water and stir gently.

3. Garnish with a cherry tomato and basil leaf.

Serving Suggestions:

Serve in a highball glass with a cherry tomato and basil leaf for garnish.

Cucumber Dill Spritzer

Description:

A refreshing, spa-like drink with a savory twist.

Calories - 60

Ingredients:

- 2 oz cucumber juice
- 1 oz dill simple syrup
- 1/2 oz lime juice
- Pinch of sea salt
- 3 oz soda water
- Ice
- Cucumber ribbon and dill sprig for garnish

Steps:

1. Combine cucumber juice, dill syrup, lime juice, and salt in a shaker with ice.
2. Shake well and strain into a glass filled with ice. Top with soda water and stir gently.
3. Garnish with a cucumber ribbon and dill sprig.

Serving Suggestions:

Serve in a highball glass with a cucumber ribbon and dill sprig for garnish.

Smoky Corn & Jalapeno Cooler

Description:

A unique, smoky-spicy drink inspired by Mexican street corn.

Ingredients:

- 2 oz grilled corn juice (blend grilled corn kernels with water and strain)
- 1/2 oz jalapeño simple syrup
- 1/2 oz lime juice
- 1/4 tsp smoked paprika
- Pinch of salt
- 2 oz soda water
- Ice
- Grilled corn kernel and jalapeño slice for garnish

Calories - 80

Steps:

1. Combine all ingredients except soda water in a shaker with ice.

2. Shake well and strain into a glass filled with ice. Top with soda water and stir gently.

3. Garnish with a grilled corn kernel and jalapeño slice.

Serving Suggestions:

Serve in a highball glass with a grilled corn kernel and jalapeño slice for garnish.

Roasted Red Pepper & Thyme Elixir

Description:

A sophisticated, savory drink with a Mediterranean flair.

Ingredients:

- 2 oz roasted red pepper puree
- 1 oz thyme simple syrup
- 1/2 oz lemon juice
- Pinch of smoked salt
- 2 oz tonic water
- Ice
- Roasted red pepper strip and thyme sprig for garnish

Calories - 70

Steps:

1. Combine red pepper puree, thyme syrup, lemon juice, and smoked salt in a shaker with ice.

2. Shake well and strain into a glass filled with ice. Top with tonic water and stir gently.

3. Garnish with a roasted red pepper strip and thyme sprig.

Serving Suggestions:

Serve in a rocks glass with a roasted red pepper strip and thyme sprig for garnish.

Celery & Green Apple Fizz

Description:

A crisp, refreshing drink with a savory-sweet balance.

Calories - 22

Ingredients:

- 2 oz celery juice
- 1 oz green apple juice
- 1/2 oz lemon juice
- 1/4 tsp celery salt
- 2 oz soda water
- Ice
- Celery stick and apple slice for garnish

Steps:

1. Combine celery juice, apple juice, lemon juice, and celery salt in a shaker with ice.
2. Shake well and strain into a glass filled with ice. Top with soda water and stir gently.
3. Garnish with a celery stick and apple slice.

Serving Suggestions:

Serve in a highball glass with a celery stick and apple slice for garnish.

Carrot Ginger Turmeric Tonic

Description:

A health-focused, savory drink with a spicy kick.

Calories - 60

Ingredients:

- 2 oz carrot juice
- 1/2 oz ginger juice
- 1/4 tsp ground turmeric
- Pinch of black pepper
- 1/2 oz lemon juice
- 2 oz coconut water
- Ice
- Carrot curl and crystallized ginger for garnish

Steps:

1. Combine all ingredients except coconut water in a shaker with ice.

2. Shake well and strain into a glass filled with ice. Top with coconut water and stir gently.

3. Garnish with a carrot curl and piece of crystallized ginger.

Serving Suggestions:

Serve in a highball glass with a carrot curl and crystallized ginger for garnish.

Mushroom & Sage Bramble

Description:

A earthy, complex drink inspired by forest flavors.

Ingredients:

- 2 oz mushroom stock (porcini or shiitake work well)
- 1/2 oz sage simple syrup
- 1/2 oz lemon juice
- 2 oz blackberry soda
- Ice
- Sage leaf and blackberry for garnish

Calories - 70

Steps:

1. Combine mushroom stock, sage syrup, and lemon juice in a shaker with ice.

2. Shake well and strain into a glass filled with crushed ice. Top with blackberry soda.

3. Garnish with a sage leaf and blackberry.

Serving Suggestions:

Serve in a rocks glass with a sage leaf and blackberry for garnish.

Gazpacho Martini

Description:

A liquid version of the classic Spanish cold soup.

Ingredients:

- 2 oz tomato juice
- 1/2 oz red bell pepper juice
- 1/4 oz cucumber juice
- 1/4 oz sherry vinegar
- Pinch of garlic powder and smoked paprika
- Ice
- Cherry tomato and cucumber slice for garnish

Calories - 40

Steps:

1. Combine all ingredients in a shaker with ice.

2. Shake well and strain into a chilled martini glass.

3. Garnish with a cherry tomato and cucumber slice on a cocktail pick.

Serving Suggestions:

Serve in a martini glass with a cherry tomato and cucumber slice on a cocktail pick.

Rosemary & Olive Brine Sparkler

Description:

A Mediterranean-inspired drink with briny, herbal notes.

Calories - 40

Ingredients:

- 1 oz olive brine
- 1/2 oz rosemary simple syrup
- 1/2 oz lemon juice
- 3 oz soda water
- Ice
- Rosemary sprig and olive for garnish

Serving Suggestions:

Serve in a highball glass with a carrot curl and crystallized ginger for garnish.

Steps:

1. Combine olive brine, rosemary syrup, and lemon juice in a shaker with ice.

2. Shake well and strain into a glass filled with ice. Top with soda water and stir gently.

3. Garnish with a rosemary sprig and olive.

Kimchi Mary

Description:

A Korean-inspired twist on a Bloody Mary.

Calories - 50

Ingredients:

- 2 oz tomato juice
- 1 oz kimchi juice (from kimchi jar)
- 1/2 oz lime juice
- 1/4 tsp gochugaru (Korean red pepper flakes)
- Dash of fish sauce
- Ice
- Kimchi and lime wheel for garnish

Steps:

1. Combine all ingredients except garnishes in a shaker with ice.
2. Shake well and strain into a glass filled with ice.
3. Garnish with a piece of kimchi and a lime wheel.

Serving Suggestions:

Serve in a highball glass with a piece of kimchi and a lime wheel for garnish.

Matcha Mint Zing

Energy Boosting Mocktails

Yerba Mate Citrus Cooler

Matcha Mint Zing

Description:

A refreshing, antioxidant-rich drink that provides a gentle caffeine boost.

Calories - 70

Ingredients:

- 1 tsp matcha powder
- 1 oz honey syrup
- 1/2 oz lime juice
- 5-6 mint leaves
- 3 oz cold water
- Ice
- Mint sprig and lime wheel for garnish

Low Calorie Alternative:
Use a zero-calorie sweetener instead of honey syrup.

Steps:

1. Whisk matcha powder with a small amount of hot water to form a paste.
2. In a shaker, muddle mint leaves with honey syrup.
3. Add matcha paste, lime juice, cold water, and ice. Shake vigorously.
4. Strain into a glass filled with ice. Garnish with a mint sprig and lime wheel.

Serving Suggestions:

Serve in a tall glass with a mint sprig and lime wheel for garnish.

Ginger Turmeric Energizer

Description:

A spicy, warming drink that aids digestion and reduces inflammation.

Calories - 90

Ingredients:

- 1 oz fresh ginger juice
- 1/4 tsp ground turmeric
- 1 oz lemon juice
- 1 oz honey
- Pinch of black pepper
- 3 oz sparkling water
- Ice
- Lemon slice and candied ginger for garnish

Low Calorie Alternative:

Use a zero-calorie sweetener instead of honey.

Steps:

1. Combine ginger juice, turmeric, lemon juice, honey, and black pepper in a shaker with ice.

2. Shake well and strain into a glass filled with ice. Top with sparkling water and stir gently.

3. Garnish with a lemon slice and piece of candied ginger.

Serving Suggestions:

Serve in a rocks glass with a lemon slice and candied ginger for garnish.

Berry Beet Blast

Description:

A vibrant, nutrient-packed drink that supports circulation and stamina.

Ingredients:

- 2 oz beet juice
- 1 oz mixed berry puree
- 1/2 oz lime juice
- 1 tsp chia seeds
- 3 oz coconut water
- Ice
- Fresh berries for garnish

Calories - 100

Steps:

1. Combine all ingredients except coconut water in a shaker with ice.

2. Shake vigorously and strain into a glass filled with ice.

3. Top with coconut water and stir gently. Garnish with fresh berries.

Low Calorie Alternative:

Use a zero-calorie sweetener instead of honey.

Serving Suggestions:

Serve in a highball glass with a blackberry and slice of lime.

Green Tea Citrus Refresh

Description:

A light, citrusy drink with a gentle caffeine boost from green tea.

Ingredients:

- 3 oz cold-brewed green tea
- 1 oz orange juice
- 1/2 oz lemon juice
- 1/2 oz honey
- 2 oz sparkling water
- Ice
- Orange slice and lemon twist for garnish

Calories - 70

Steps:

1. Combine green tea, orange juice, lemon juice, and honey in a shaker with ice.

2. Shake well and strain into a glass filled with ice. Top with sparkling water and stir gently.

3. Garnish with an orange slice and lemon twist.

Low Calorie Alternative:

Use a zero-calorie sweetener instead of honey.

Serving Suggestions:

Serve in a highball glass with an orange slice and lemon twist for garnish.

Espresso Coconut Cooler

Description:

A creamy, coffee-based drink that provides a significant energy boost.

Calories - 120

Ingredients:

- 2 oz cold brew coffee concentrate
- 2 oz coconut milk
- 1/2 oz maple syrup
- 1/4 tsp vanilla extract
- Ice
- Cocoa powder for dusting

Steps:

1. Combine all ingredients in a shaker with ice.
2. Shake vigorously until frothy. Strain into a glass filled with ice.
3. Dust with cocoa powder.

Low Calorie Alternative:

Use a zero-calorie sweetener instead of maple syrup.

Serving Suggestions:

Serve in a highball glass dusted with cocoa powder.

Watermelon Basil Energizer

Description:

A hydrating, electrolyte-rich drink that's perfect for post-workout recovery.

Calories - 60

Ingredients:

- 3 oz fresh watermelon juice
- 5-6 basil leaves
- 1/2 oz lime juice
- 1/4 tsp sea salt
- 2 oz coconut water
- Ice
- Watermelon wedge and basil leaf for garnish

Steps:

1. Muddle basil leaves in a shaker. Add watermelon juice, lime juice, salt, and ice. Shake well.
2. Strain into a glass filled with ice. Top with coconut water and stir gently.
3. Garnish with a watermelon wedge and basil leaf.

Serving Suggestions:

Serve in a highball glass with a watermelon wedge and basil leaf for garnish.

Maca Cacao Power Shake

Description:

A rich, chocolatey drink with maca for sustained energy.

Ingredients:

- 1 tsp maca powder
- 1 tsp raw cacao powder
- 1 banana
- 1 cup almond milk
- 1/2 tsp vanilla extract
- Ice
- Cacao nibs for garnish

Calories - 150

Steps:

1. Blend all ingredients except cacao nibs until smooth.
2. Pour into a glass.
3. Sprinkle with cacao nibs.

Low Calorie Alternative:

Use a zero-calorie sweetener instead of vanilla extract.

Serving Suggestions:

Serve in a smoothie glass sprinkled with cacao nibs.

Guarana Berry Boost

Description:

A fruity drink with a natural caffeine kick from guarana.

Ingredients:

- 1/2 tsp guarana powder
- 2 oz mixed berry juice
- 1 oz pomegranate juice
- 1/2 oz lemon juice
- 1 tsp honey
- 2 oz sparkling water
- Ice
- Mixed berries for garnish

Calories - 80

Steps:

1. Combine all ingredients except sparkling water in a shaker with ice.

2. Shake well and strain into a glass filled with ice.

3. Top with sparkling water and stir gently. Garnish with mixed berries.

Low Calorie Alternative:

Use a zero-calorie sweetener instead of honey.

Serving Suggestions:

Serve in a highball glass with mixed berries for garnish.

Yerba Mate Citrus Cooler

Description:

A refreshing drink featuring yerba mate, known for its smooth energy boost.

Calories - 70

Ingredients:

- 3 oz cold-brewed yerba mate
- 1 oz grapefruit juice
- 1/2 oz lime juice
- 1/2 oz agave syrup
- 2 oz soda water
- Ice
- Grapefruit wedge and lime wheel for garnish

Serving Suggestions:

Serve in a highball glass with a grapefruit wedge and lime wheel for garnish.

Steps:

1. Combine yerba mate, grapefruit juice, lime juice, and agave syrup in a shaker with ice.

2. Shake well and strain into a glass filled with ice. Top with soda water and stir gently.

3. Garnish with a grapefruit wedge and lime wheel.

Low Calorie Alternative:

Use a zero-calorie sweetener instead of agave syrup.

Acai Pomegranate Power Punch

Description:

A antioxidant-rich, fruity drink that provides lasting energy.

Calories - 100

Ingredients:

- 2 oz acai berry puree
- 1 oz pomegranate juice
- 1/2 oz lemon juice
- 1 tsp honey
- 2 oz green tea (cold)
- Ice
- Pomegranate seeds for garnish

Serving Suggestions:

Serve in a highball glass with pomegranate seeds for garnish.

Steps:

1. Combine all ingredients except green tea in a shaker with ice.

2. Shake vigorously and strain into a glass filled with ice.

3. Top with cold green tea and stir gently. Sprinkle pomegranate seeds on top.

Low Calorie Alternative:

Use a zero-calorie sweetener instead of honey.

Virgin Sea Breeze

Classic Mocktails

Virgin Mojito

Virgin Mojito

Description:

A refreshing blend of zesty lime, cool mint, and effervescent soda water. The sweetness of the syrup balances the tartness of lime, while mint adds a fresh, aromatic touch.

Ingredients:

- 8-10 mint leaves
- 1 oz simple syrup
- 1 oz lime juice
- 2 oz soda water
- Ice

Calories - 70

Steps:

1. Muddle mint leaves with simple syrup in a glass.

2. Add lime juice and ice. Top with soda water and stir gently.

3. Garnish with mint sprig and lime wheel.

Low Calorie Alternative:

Use a zero-calorie sweetener instead of simple syrup.

Serving Suggestions:

Serve in a highball glass with a metal straw. Garnish with a mint sprig and lime wheel.

Shirley Temple

Description:

A classic mocktail that combines the spicy sweetness of ginger ale with the fruity notes of grenadine. The carbonation provides a pleasant fizz, while the grenadine adds both flavor and a beautiful color.

Ingredients:

- 4 oz ginger ale
- 1/2 oz grenadine
- Ice

Calories - 100

Steps:

1. Fill glass with ice and pour in ginger ale.

2. Add grenadine and stir gently.

3. Garnish with a maraschino cherry.

Low Calorie Alternative:

Use diet ginger ale and sugar-free grenadine.

Serving Suggestions:

Serve in a collins glass. Garnish with a maraschino cherry and an orange slice.

Virgin Pina Colada

Description:

A tropical delight that blends the sweetness of pineapple with the creamy richness of coconut. The lime juice adds a subtle tartness that balances the drink's sweetness.

Calories - 250

Ingredients:

- 3 oz pineapple juice
- 2 oz coconut cream
- 1/2 oz lime juice
- Ice

Low Calorie Alternative:

Use light coconut milk instead of coconut cream and reduce pineapple juice to 2 oz.

Steps:

1. Blend all ingredients with ice until smooth.
2. Pour into a glass.
3. Garnish with a pineapple wedge and cherry.

Serving Suggestions:

Serve in a hurricane glass. Garnish with a pineapple wedge, cherry, and paper umbrella.

Virgin Mary

Description:

A savory mocktail that combines tangy tomato juice with a blend of spices. Worcestershire sauce adds depth, while hot sauce provides a spicy kick.

Calories - 50

Ingredients:

- 4 oz tomato juice
- 1/2 oz lemon juice
- 2 dashes Worcestershire sauce
- 2 dashes hot sauce
- Pinch of salt and pepper
- Celery salt for rimming
- Ice

Steps:

1. Rim glass with celery salt. Combine all ingredients in a shaker with ice.
2. Shake well and strain into the prepared glass over ice.
3. Garnish with celery stalk and lemon wedge.

Low Calorie Alternative:

Use low-sodium tomato juice.

Serving Suggestions:

Serve in a highball glass. Garnish with a celery stalk, lemon wedge, and cocktail olive.

Arnold Palmer

Description:

A refreshing combination of tangy lemonade and smooth iced tea. The sweetness of the lemonade complements the slight bitterness of the tea, creating a perfectly balanced drink.

Ingredients:

- 2 oz unsweetened iced tea
- 2 oz lemonade
- Ice

Calories - 50

Steps:

1. Fill glass with ice.

2. Pour in equal parts iced tea and lemonade.

3. Stir gently and garnish with a lemon wedge.

Low Calorie Alternative:

Use sugar-free lemonade.

Serving Suggestions:

Serve in a tall glass. Garnish with a lemon wheel and a sprig of mint.

Virgin Margarita

Description:

A tangy and refreshing blend that mimics the classic margarita. The lime juice provides a zesty kick, balanced by the sweetness of simple syrup, while orange juice adds depth and complexity.

Ingredients:

- 2 oz lime juice
- 1 oz simple syrup
- 1 oz orange juice
- Salt for rimming (optional)
- Ice

Calories - 70

Steps:

1. If desired, rim glass with salt.

2. Combine lime juice, simple syrup, and orange juice in a shaker with ice.

3. Shake well and strain into the prepared glass over ice. Garnish with a lime wheel.

Low Calorie Alternative:
Use a zero-calorie sweetener instead of simple syrup.

Serving Suggestions:
Serve in a margarita glass with a salted rim. Garnish with a lime wheel or wedge.

Cinderella

Description:

A fruity and vibrant mocktail that combines citrus juices with the sweetness of grenadine and the fizz of ginger ale. The mix of juices creates a complex flavor profile, while the ginger ale adds a spicy note and effervescence.

Calories - 120

Ingredients:

- 1 oz lemon juice
- 1 oz orange juice
- 1 oz pineapple juice
- 1/2 oz grenadine
- 2 oz ginger ale
- Ice

Low Calorie Alternative:

Use low-sodium tomato juice.

Serving Suggestions:

Serve in a hurricane glass. Garnish with an orange slice and a maraschino cherry.

Steps:

1. Combine juices and grenadine in a shaker with ice.

2. Shake well and strain into a glass filled with ice. Top with ginger ale and stir gently.

3. Garnish with an orange slice and cherry.

Virgin Cucumber Gimlet

Description:

A crisp and refreshing mocktail that highlights the clean flavor of cucumber. The lime juice adds brightness, while the simple syrup balances the tartness, resulting in a sophisticated and cooling drink.

Calories - 50

Ingredients:

- 2 oz cucumber juice
- 1 oz lime juice
- 1/2 oz simple syrup
- Ice

Low Calorie Alternative:

Use a zero-calorie sweetener instead of simple syrup.

Steps:

1. Combine all ingredients in a shaker with ice.

2. Shake well and strain into a chilled glass.

3. Garnish with a cucumber slice.

Serving Suggestions:

Serve in a chilled coupe or martini glass. Garnish with a thin cucumber slice or ribbon.

Virgin Mint Julep

Description:

A refreshing mocktail that captures the essence of the classic julep. The mint provides a cool, aromatic flavor, while the apple juice adds sweetness and body. The crushed ice creates a frosty, slushy texture.

Ingredients:

- 8-10 mint leaves
- 1 oz simple syrup
- 2 oz apple juice
- Crushed ice

Calories - 80

Steps:

1. Muddle mint leaves with simple syrup in a julep cup or glass.
2. Fill the glass with crushed ice. Pour in apple juice and stir until the outside of the glass frosts.
3. Garnish with a mint sprig.

Low Calorie Alternative:

Use a zero-calorie sweetener instead of simple syrup and unsweetened apple juice.

Serving Suggestions:

Serve in a silver julep cup or a rocks glass. Garnish with a generous mint sprig.

Virgin Sea Breeze

Description:

A tart and fruity mocktail that combines the boldness of cranberry with the citrusy notes of grapefruit and lime. The mix of juices creates a well-balanced drink with a refreshing finish.

Ingredients:

- 3 oz cranberry juice
- 1.5 oz grapefruit juice
- 1/2 oz lime juice
- Ice

Calories - 70

Steps:

1. Combine all juices in a shaker with ice.

2. Shake well and strain into a glass filled with ice.

3. Garnish with a lime wheel.

Low Calorie Alternative:

Use diet cranberry juice and fresh grapefruit juice to reduce sugar content.

Serving Suggestions:

Serve in a highball glass. Garnish with a lime wheel and a grapefruit wedge.

Roy Rogers

Description:

The Roy Rogers is a classic, non-alcoholic mocktail that combines the deep, rich flavor of cola with the sweet, fruity notes of grenadine.

Calories - 67

Ingredients:

- 4 oz cola
- 1/2 oz grenadine
- Ice
- Maraschino cherry for garnish

Low Calorie Alternative:

Use diet cola and sugar-free grenadine.

Steps:

1. Fill glass with ice and pour in cola.
2. Add grenadine and stir gently.
3. Garnish with a maraschino cherry.

Serving Suggestions:

Serve in a highball glass with a maraschino cherry for garnish.

Virgin Sangria

Description:

The Virgin Sangria is a vibrant and refreshing non-alcoholic twist on the classic Spanish drink. This delightful concoction brings together the sweetness of the juices and the tartness of the fruits, creating a perfectly balanced and visually stunning beverage.

Calories - 79

Ingredients:

- 2 oz grape juice
- 1 oz orange juice
- 1 oz apple juice
- 1/2 oz lemon juice
- Assorted fresh fruit (orange slices, apple chunks, grapes)
- Ice
- Splash of soda water

Low Calorie Alternative:

Use diet cola and sugar-free grenadine.

Steps:

1. Combine all juices in a pitcher with fresh fruit.
2. Chill for at least an hour.
3. Serve over ice and top with a splash of soda water.

Serving Suggestions:

Serve in a wine glass with assorted fresh fruit for garnish.

Shirly Ginger

Description:

The Shirley Ginger is a delightful and spicy twist on the classic Shirley Temple mocktail. Combining the zesty kick of ginger beer with the sweetness of grenadine and a splash of lime juice, this drink offers a perfect balance of flavors.

Ingredients:

- 4 oz ginger beer
- 1/2 oz lime juice
- 1/4 oz grenadine
- Ice
- Lime wheel for garnish

Calories - 90

Low Calorie Alternative:

Use diet ginger beer and sugar-free grenadine.

Serving Suggestions:

Serve in a rocks glass with a lime wheel for garnish.

Steps:

1 Fill glass with ice.

2 Add ginger beer, lime juice, and grenadine.

3 Stir gently and garnish with a lime wheel.

Virgin Colada Sunrise

Description:

The Virgin Colada Sunrise is a tropical paradise in a glass, blending the creamy richness of coconut cream with the bright, sweet flavor of pineapple juice. A splash of orange juice and a drizzle of grenadine create a stunning sunrise effect, making this mocktail as beautiful as it is delicious.

Ingredients:

- 2 oz pineapple juice
- 1 oz coconut cream
- 1/2 oz orange juice
- 1/2 oz grenadine
- Ice
- Pineapple wedge and cherry for garnish

Calories - 155

Steps:

1. Combine pineapple juice, coconut cream, and orange juice in a shaker with ice.

2. Shake well and strain into a glass filled with ice.

3. Slowly pour grenadine down the side of the glass to create a "sunrise" effect.

3. Garnish with pineapple wedge and cherry.

Low Calorie Alternative:

Use light coconut milk and sugar-free grenadine.

Serving Suggestions:

Serve in a hurricane glass with a pineapple wedge and cherry for garnish.

Nojito
(Non-Alcoholic Mojito)

Description:

The Nojito is a refreshing and minty mocktail that captures all the flavors of a traditional Mojito without the alcohol. The Nojito's crisp, clean taste makes it a versatile option that pairs well with a variety of cuisines, ensuring it will be a hit at any gathering.

Calories - 90

Ingredients:

- 8-10 mint leaves
- 1 oz lime juice
- 1 oz simple syrup
- 2 oz apple juice
- 1 oz soda water
- Ice
- Mint sprig and lime wheel for garnish

Steps:

1. Muddle mint leaves with lime juice and simple syrup in a glass.
2. Add apple juice and ice. Top with soda water and stir gently.
3. Garnish with mint sprig and lime wheel.

Low Calorie Alternative:

Use a zero-calorie sweetener instead of simple syrup.

Serving Suggestions:

Serve in a highball glass with a mint sprig and lime wheel for garnish.

Virgin Colada Sunrise

Strawberry Cheesecake Cooler

Dessert-Inspired Mocktails

Pistachio Rosewater Dream

Chocolate Brownie Skake

Description:

This indulgent mocktail combines rich chocolate flavors with a hint of coffee, mimicking a fudgy brownie. The vanilla adds depth, while the milk creates a creamy texture.

Calories - 250

Ingredients:

- 2 oz chocolate syrup
- 1 oz espresso (cold)
- 4 oz milk
- 1/4 tsp vanilla extract
- Ice
- Whipped cream and chocolate shavings for garnish

Low Calorie Alternative:

Use sugar-free chocolate syrup and skim milk.

Steps:

1. Blend all ingredients except garnishes with ice until smooth.
2. Pour into a glass and top with whipped cream and chocolate shavings.

Serving Suggestions:

Serve in a milkshake glass with a wide straw. Rim the glass with chocolate sauce and cookie crumbs.

Key Lime Pie Fizz

Description:

This zesty mocktail captures the tangy-sweet flavor of key lime pie. The graham cracker rim adds texture, while the fizzy water lightens the drink.

Calories - 200

Ingredients:

- 2 oz lime juice
- 1 oz sweetened condensed milk
- 1 oz heavy cream
- 2 oz soda water
- Ice
- Graham cracker crumbs for rim

Steps:

1. Rim glass with graham cracker crumbs.
2. Shake lime juice, condensed milk, and cream with ice.
3. Strain into the prepared glass over fresh ice. Top with soda water and stir gently.

Low Calorie Alternative:

Use fat-free condensed milk and replace heavy cream with almond milk.

Serving Suggestions:

Serve in a rocks glass. Garnish with a lime wheel and a dollop of whipped cream.

Strawberry Cheesecake Cooler

Description:

This creamy mocktail embodies the rich, fruity flavor of strawberry cheesecake. The cream cheese provides authenticity, while the graham cracker garnish adds a crust-like element.

Ingredients:

- 2 oz strawberry puree
- 1 oz cream cheese, softened
- 1 oz vanilla syrup
- 3 oz milk
- Ice
- Whipped cream and graham cracker for garnish

Calories - 300

Steps:

1. Blend all ingredients except garnishes until smooth.
2. Pour into a glass filled with ice.
3. Top with whipped cream and crushed graham cracker.

Low Calorie Alternative:

Use low-fat cream cheese and sugar-free vanilla syrup.

Serving Suggestions:

Serve in a mason jar. Garnish with a strawberry and a graham cracker stick.

Tiramisu Delight

Description:

This mocktail captures the coffee and cocoa notes of tiramisu. The mascarpone adds richness, while the soda water provides a light, bubbly finish.

Ingredients:

- 2 oz cold espresso
- 1 oz mascarpone cheese
- 1/2 oz vanilla syrup
- 2 oz milk
- 1 oz soda water
- Ice
- Cocoa powder for dusting

Calories - 200

Steps:

1. Blend espresso, mascarpone, vanilla syrup, and milk until smooth.

2. Pour over ice in a glass.

3. Top with soda water and dust with cocoa powder.

Low Calorie Alternative:

Use low-fat mascarpone and sugar-free vanilla syrup.

Serving Suggestions:

Serve in a small wine glass or coupe. Garnish with a sprinkle of cocoa powder and a coffee bean.

Apple Pie
A La Mode

Description:

This mocktail combines the warm spices of apple pie with the creamy sweetness of vanilla ice cream. The carbonation adds a playful twist to this classic dessert combination.

Calories - 250

Ingredients:

- 3 oz apple juice
- 1/2 tsp ground cinnamon
- 1 oz vanilla syrup
- 1 oz heavy cream
- 2 oz ginger ale
- Ice
- Whipped cream and cinnamon stick for garnish

Low Calorie Alternative:

Use sugar-free vanilla syrup and replace heavy cream with almond milk.

Steps:

1. Shake apple juice, cinnamon, vanilla syrup, and cream with ice.

2. Strain into a glass filled with fresh ice. Top with ginger ale and stir gently.

3. Garnish with whipped cream and a cinnamon stick.

Serving Suggestions:

Serve in a highball glass. Garnish with a thin apple slice and a sprinkle of cinnamon.

Banana Split Smoothie

Description:

This creamy mocktail captures the essence of a classic banana split. The blend of banana, strawberry, and chocolate mimics the traditional sundae flavors, while the milk provides a smooth, ice cream-like texture.

Calories - 300

Ingredients:

- 1 ripe banana
- 2 oz strawberry puree
- 1 oz chocolate syrup
- 4 oz milk
- Ice
- Whipped cream, cherry, and crushed peanuts for garnish

Low Calorie Alternative:

Use sugar-free chocolate syrup and skim milk.

Steps:

1. Blend banana, strawberry puree, chocolate syrup, and milk with ice until smooth.
2. Pour into a glass and top with whipped cream.
2. Garnish with a cherry and sprinkle of crushed peanuts.

Serving Suggestions:

Serve in a sundae glass. Add a colorful straw and a long spoon for the full sundae experience.

Lemon Meringue Fizz

Description:

This bright, citrusy mocktail embodies the flavors of lemon meringue pie. The lemon curd provides richness, while the fizzy water mimics the light texture of meringue.

Ingredients:

- 1 oz lemon curd
- 1 oz lemon juice
- 1/2 oz vanilla syrup
- 2 oz milk
- 2 oz soda water
- Ice
- Meringue cookie for garnish

Calories - 200

Steps:

1. Shake lemon curd, lemon juice, vanilla syrup, and milk with ice.

2. Strain into a glass filled with fresh ice. Top with soda water and stir gently.

3. Garnish with a meringue cookie.

Low Calorie Alternative:

Use sugar-free vanilla syrup and skim milk.

Serving Suggestions:

Serve in a coupe glass. Garnish with a lemon twist and a small meringue cookie on the rim.

Peaches & Cream Cooler

Description:

This smooth, fruity mocktail recreates the classic peaches and cream dessert. The peach nectar provides a natural sweetness, while the cream adds a luxurious texture.

Ingredients:

- 3 oz peach nectar
- 1 oz vanilla syrup
- 2 oz heavy cream
- 1 oz milk
- Ice
- Whipped cream and peach slice for garnish

Calories - 250

Steps:

1. Shake all ingredients except garnishes with ice.

2. Strain into a glass filled with fresh ice.

3. Top with whipped cream and garnish with a peach slice.

Low Calorie Alternative:

Use sugar-free vanilla syrup and replace heavy cream with almond milk.

Serving Suggestions:

Serve in a hurricane glass. Garnish with a fresh peach slice and a sprinkle of cinnamon.

S'mores Shake

Description:

This indulgent mocktail brings the campfire favorite to your glass. The combination of chocolate and marshmallow captures the essence of s'mores, while the graham cracker rim adds the crucial crunch.

Calories - 350

Ingredients:

- 2 oz chocolate syrup
- 1 oz marshmallow fluff
- 4 oz milk
- Ice
- Graham cracker crumbs for rim
- Whipped cream and mini marshmallows for garnish

Low Calorie Alternative:

Use sugar-free chocolate syrup and skim milk.

Steps:

1. Rim glass with graham cracker crumbs.
2. Blend chocolate syrup, marshmallow fluff, and milk with ice until smooth.
3. Pour into the prepared glass. Top with whipped cream and mini marshmallows

Serving Suggestions:

Serve in a milkshake glass. Garnish with a toasted marshmallow on a skewer.

Pistachio Rosewater Dream

Description:

This unique mocktail is inspired by Middle Eastern desserts. The pistachio provides a nutty base, while the rosewater adds a delicate floral note, creating a sophisticated and dreamy blend.

Calories - 200

Ingredients:

- 2 oz pistachio milk (or almond milk blended with 1 tbsp pistachio paste)
- 1/2 oz rosewater
- 1 oz simple syrup
- 2 oz milk
- Ice
- Crushed pistachios and dried rose petals for garnish

Low Calorie Alternative:

Use sugar-free chocolate syrup and skim milk.

Steps:

1. Shake all ingredients except garnishes with ice.
2. Strain into a glass filled with fresh ice.
3. Garnish with crushed pistachios and rose petals.

Serving Suggestions:

Serve in a milkshake glass. Garnish with a toasted marshmallow on a skewer.

Sage & Blackberry Smash

Herbal Mocktails

Chamomile Honey Elixir

Lavender Lemon Fizz

Description:

This refreshing mocktail combines the floral notes of lavender with zesty lemon. The honey adds sweetness, while the soda water provides a light, effervescent finish.

Calories - 100

Ingredients:

- 1 oz lavender syrup
- 1 oz fresh lemon juice
- 1/2 oz honey
- 3 oz soda water
- Ice
- Lavender sprig and lemon wheel for garnish

Low Calorie Alternative:

Use sugar-free lavender syrup and replace honey with a zero-calorie sweetener.

Steps:

1. Combine lavender syrup, lemon juice, and honey in a shaker with ice.
2. Shake well and strain into a glass filled with ice. Top with soda water and stir gently.
3. Garnish with a lavender sprig and lemon wheel.

Serving Suggestions:

Serve in a highball glass. Garnish with a lavender sprig and a thin lemon wheel.

Basil Cucumber Cooler

Description:

This refreshing mocktail combines the cooling properties of cucumber with the aromatic flavor of basil. The lime adds a zesty kick, creating a perfectly balanced summer drink.

Calories - 80

Ingredients:

- 2 oz cucumber juice
- 1 oz basil simple syrup
- 1/2 oz lime juice
- 3 oz soda water
- Ice
- Cucumber ribbon and basil leaves for garnish

Low Calorie Alternative:

Use sugar-free basil syrup.

Serving Suggestions:

Serve in a collins glass. Garnish with a long cucumber ribbon and a bouquet of basil leaves.

Steps:

1. Muddle a few basil leaves in a shaker. Add cucumber juice, basil syrup, and lime juice with ice.

2. Shake well and strain into a glass filled with ice. Top with soda water and stir gently.

3. Garnish with a cucumber ribbon and fresh basil leaves.

Thyme & Elderflower Spritz

Description:

This elegant mocktail combines the subtle, earthy notes of thyme with the delicate sweetness of elderflower. The lemon adds brightness, while the tonic water provides a pleasant bitterness and effervescence.

Ingredients:

- 1 oz thyme simple syrup
- 1 oz elderflower cordial
- 1/2 oz lemon juice
- 3 oz tonic water
- Ice
- Thyme sprig and lemon twist for garnish

Calories - 100

Steps:

1. Combine thyme syrup, elderflower cordial, and lemon juice in a shaker with ice.
2. Shake well and strain into a glass filled with ice. Top with tonic water and stir gently.
3. Garnish with a thyme sprig and lemon twist.

Low Calorie Alternative:

Use sugar-free thyme syrup and diet tonic water.

Serving Suggestions:

Serve in a wine glass. Garnish with a lemon twist wrapped around a fresh thyme sprig.

Mint Matcha Iced Tea

Description:

This refreshing mocktail combines the earthy flavor of matcha with the cooling effect of mint. The honey adds sweetness, while the ice creates a refreshing, slushy texture.

Ingredients:

- 1 tsp matcha powder
- 1 oz mint simple syrup
- 4 oz cold water
- 1/2 oz honey
- Ice
- Fresh mint leaves for garnish

Calories - 90

Steps:

1. Whisk matcha powder with a small amount of hot water to form a paste.

2. In a shaker, combine matcha paste, mint syrup, cold water, and honey with ice.

3. Shake vigorously and pour (unstrained) into a glass. Garnish with fresh mint leaves.

Low Calorie Alternative:

Use sugar-free mint syrup and replace honey with a zero-calorie sweetener.

Serving Suggestions:

Serve in a tall glass. Garnish with a bouquet of fresh mint leaves and a matcha-dusted rim.

Sage & Blackberry Smash

Description:

This sophisticated mocktail combines the earthy, slightly peppery flavor of sage with the sweet-tart taste of blackberries. The lemon adds brightness, while the honey balances the flavors.

Calories - 110

Ingredients:

- 6-8 fresh blackberries
- 3-4 sage leaves
- 1 oz lemon juice
- 1 oz honey syrup
- 2 oz soda water
- Ice
- Sage leaf and blackberry for garnish

Low Calorie Alternative:

Use a zero-calorie sweetener instead of honey syrup.

Steps:

1. Muddle blackberries and sage leaves in a shaker. Add lemon juice, honey syrup, and ice. Shake vigorously.

2. Double strain into a glass filled with ice. Top with soda water and stir gently.

3. Garnish with a sage leaf and a blackberry.

Serving Suggestions:

Serve in a rocks glass. Garnish with a fresh sage leaf and a skewered blackberry.

Cilantro Lime Cooler

Description:

This refreshing mocktail showcases the bright, citrusy notes of cilantro paired with zesty lime. The agave nectar adds sweetness, while the sparkling water provides a crisp finish.

Calories - 80

Ingredients:

- 1/4 cup fresh cilantro leaves
- 1 oz lime juice
- 1 oz agave nectar
- 3 oz sparkling water
- Ice
- Cilantro sprig and lime wheel for garnish

Low Calorie Alternative:

Use a zero-calorie sweetener instead of agave nectar.

Steps:

1. Muddle cilantro leaves in a shaker. Add lime juice, agave nectar, and ice. Shake well.

2. Double strain into a glass filled with ice. Top with sparkling water and stir gently.

3. Garnish with a cilantro sprig and lime wheel.

Serving Suggestions:

Serve in a collins glass. Garnish with a cilantro sprig and a thin lime wheel.

Chamomile Honey Elixir

Description:

This soothing mocktail combines the calming properties of chamomile with the sweetness of honey. The lemon adds a gentle acidity, while the vanilla provides depth and warmth.

Ingredients:

- 3 oz strong-brewed chamomile tea, cooled
- 1 oz honey
- 1/2 oz lemon juice
- 1/4 tsp vanilla extract
- 2 oz soda water
- Ice
- Chamomile flowers for garnish (if available)

Calories - 90

Steps:

1. Combine chamomile tea, honey, lemon juice, and vanilla in a shaker with ice.

2. Shake well and strain into a glass filled with ice. Top with soda water and stir gently.

3. Garnish with chamomile flowers if available.

Low Calorie Alternative:

Use a zero-calorie sweetener instead of honey.

Serving Suggestions:

Serve in a teacup or small glass. Garnish with dried chamomile flowers or a lemon twist.

Lemongrass Ginger Fizz

Description:

This invigorating mocktail combines the citrusy, floral notes of lemongrass with the spicy warmth of ginger. The lime adds brightness, while the sparkling water provides a refreshing effervescence.

Ingredients:

- 2 oz lemongrass syrup
- 1 oz fresh ginger juice
- 1/2 oz lime juice
- 3 oz sparkling water
- Ice
- Lemongrass stalk and lime wedge for garnish

Calories - 100

Steps:

1. Combine lemongrass syrup, ginger juice, and lime juice in a shaker with ice.

2. Shake well and strain into a glass filled with ice. Top with sparkling water and stir gently.

3. Garnish with a lemongrass stalk and lime wedge.

Low Calorie Alternative:

Use sugar-free lemongrass syrup.

Serving Suggestions:

Serve in a highball glass. Garnish with a lemongrass stalk used as a stirrer and a lime wedge

Hibiscus Rose Cooler

Description:

This floral mocktail combines the tart, berry-like flavor of hibiscus with the delicate essence of rose. The honey adds sweetness, while the sparkling water lightens the drink.

Calories - 80

Ingredients:

- 2 oz hibiscus tea, cooled
- 1 oz rose water
- 1 oz honey syrup
- 2 oz sparkling water
- Ice
- Dried hibiscus flowers and rose petals for garnish

Low Calorie Alternative:

Use a zero-calorie sweetener instead of honey syrup.

Steps:

1. Combine hibiscus tea, rose water, and honey syrup in a shaker with ice.
2. Shake well and strain into a glass filled with ice. Top with sparkling water and stir gently.
3. Garnish with dried hibiscus flowers and rose petals.

Serving Suggestions:

Serve in a wine glass. Float dried hibiscus flowers and rose petals on top for a visually stunning presentation

Fennel & Green Apple Refresher

Description:

This unique mocktail combines the crisp, anise-like flavor of fennel with the tart sweetness of green apple. The lemon adds brightness, while the honey provides balance.

Calories - 100

Ingredients:

- 2 oz fresh fennel juice (from about 1/2 bulb of fennel)
- 2 oz green apple juice
- 1/2 oz lemon juice
- 1/2 oz honey
- 2 oz sparkling water
- Ice
- Thinly sliced fennel and green apple fan for garnish

Serving Suggestions:

Serve in a wine glass. Float dried hibiscus flowers and rose petals on top for a visually stunning presentation

Steps:

1. Combine fennel juice, green apple juice, lemon juice, and honey in a shaker with ice.

2. Shake vigorously for about 15 seconds. Strain into a glass filled with ice Top with sparkling water and stir gently.

3. Garnish with a thinly sliced piece of fennel and a fan of green apple.

Low Calorie Alternative:

Use a zero-calorie sweetener instead of honey syrup.

Cardamon Pear Sparkler

Description:

This elegant mocktail combines the warm, aromatic spice of cardamom with the delicate sweetness of pear.

Ingredients:

- 2 oz pear nectar
- 1 oz cardamom simple syrup
- 1/2 oz lemon juice
- 1/4 oz honey
- 2 oz sparkling water
- Ice
- Thinly sliced pear and a few cardamom pods for garnish

Calories - 90

Steps:

1. To make cardamom simple syrup, simmer equal parts sugar and water with crushed cardamom pods, then strain and cool.

2. Combine pear nectar, cardamom syrup, lemon juice, and honey in a shaker with ice.

3. Shake vigorously for about 15 seconds. Strain into a glass filled with ice.

4. Top with sparkling water and stir gently. Garnish with a thin pear slice and a few cardamom pods.

Low Calorie Alternative:

Use a zero-calorie sweetener instead of honey.

Serving Suggestions:

Serve in a teacup or small glass. Garnish with dried chamomile flowers or a lemon twist.

Other Books by Jeffrey C. Chapman

Our catalog is constantly growing!

Visit AdultingHardBooks.com

Made in the USA
Las Vegas, NV
27 October 2024